RHS

THIS DIARY BELONGS TO...

NAME:

ADDRESS:

POSTCODE:

TELEPHONE:

WORK:

MOBILE:

E-MAIL:

IN AN EMERGENCY...

NAME:

ADDRESS:

POSTCODE:

WORK:

MOBILE:

ABOUT US

The Royal Horticultural Society (RHS) was founded in 1804 and is the UK's largest gardening charity. The RHS vision is to enrich everyone's life through plants and make the UK a greener and more beautiful place via its inspirational gardens and shows, science research and advisory, extensive library collections and far-reaching education and community programmes. With over 600,000 members the RHS also shares its horticultural knowledge and expertise with millions of people every year through its website and publications.

In 2021, the RHS launched its Sustainability Strategy, committing to be net positive for nature and people by 2030. The supporting RHS Planet-Friendly Gardening Campaign will continue to harness the power of the UK's 30 million gardeners to help tackle the climate and biodiversity crisis.

We are solely funded by our members, visitors and supporters.
For more information visit www.rhs.org.uk

OUR GARDENS:

Our five gardens provide great days out for everyone. Each garden offers a unique experience that includes spectacular gardens with interesting walks, ample parking, cafes and restaurants, organised events, a garden centre and gift shop. To find out more about all of our gardens and what's on, visit: www.rhs.org.uk/gardens.

- RHS Garden Bridgewater, Salford, Greater Manchester M28 2LJ:
Our fifth RHS garden opened in 2021 bringing the historic gardens of Worsley New Hall back to life, providing a stunning new 62 hectare (154 acre) garden in the heart of the North West.

- RHS Garden Harlow Carr, Harrogate, North Yorkshire HG3 1QB:
Sitting in the beautiful Yorkshire countryside, Harlow Carr has a wide variety of growing landscapes, from running and still water to wildflower meadows. Visit the Alpine House and wander through the Rhododendron Glade, which is particularly beautiful in the spring.

- RHS Garden Hyde Hall, Chelmsford, Essex CM3 8RA:
Nestled in the heart of Essex, Hyde Hall has a unique character and charm. This is a dynamic garden with spectacular views that are constantly changing to meet the challenges of the open site and soil conditions.

- RHS Garden Rosemoor, Great Torrington, Devon EX38 8PH:
Set in rural North Devon, this garden is truly beautiful, situated within a steep wooded valley. Donated to the RHS in 1988, the gardens and woodland reflect the characteristic style of a West Country garden.

ABOUT US

- RHS Garden Wisley, Woking, Surrey GU23 6QB:
This is our most established garden and also the base for our scientific activity. Within the gardens you will find the spectacular Glasshouse, which provides a home to many tropical species. This garden is a great destination whatever the season.

OUR SHOWS:
RHS shows are the highlight of many a gardener's year and include the RHS Chelsea Flower Show, RHS Hampton Court Palace Garden Festival, and many more. Find the latest show dates and buy tickets at: www.rhs.org.uk/shows-events

OUR LIBRARIES:
Our libraries hold the world's finest collection of books and printed materials on gardening and outstanding collections of archives, photography and botanical art.
For enquiries about RHS libraries, email: library@rhs.org.uk
For more information,
visit: www.rhs.org.uk/education-learning/libraries-at-rhs

ADVICE:
For general, monthly and seasonal advice, information for beginners, ideas for garden designs and topical articles from our expert gardeners, visit: www.rhs.org.uk/advice

MEMBERSHIP:
Make our world-famous gardens your own with unlimited access to our five RHS Gardens. More than 200 RHS Partner Gardens across the UK for RHS main members to enjoy for free at selected times.

ABOUT US

GREAT REASONS TO JOIN:
- Visit all 5 RHS Gardens for the member and a family guest or 2 children
- Monthly subscription to The Garden magazine
- Unlimited, personalised RHS gardening advice
- Regular emails with exclusive member content
- Free entry to over 200 Partner Gardens for the member
- Savings on tickets to RHS Shows

Visit: www.rhs.org.uk/join

For membership enquiries, call 0203 176 5820
(weekdays 9am to 5pm, excluding Bank Holidays)
or email membership@rhs.org.uk

RHS

® The Royal Horticultural Society. The Royal Horticultural Society, and its logo, are trade marks of The Royal Horticultural Society (Registered Charity No 222879/SC038262) and used under licence from RHS Enterprises Limited.

CONTACT NUMBERS

NAME:

TEL:

NAME:

TEL:

NAME:

TEL:

NAME:

TEL:

NAME:

TEL:

NAME:

TEL:

NAME:

TEL:

NAME:

TEL:

NAME:

TEL:

NAME:

TEL:

CONTACT NUMBERS

NAME:

TEL:

NAME:

TEL:

NAME:

TEL:

NAME:

TEL:

NAME:

TEL:

NAME:

TEL:

NAME:

TEL:

NAME:

TEL:

NAME:

TEL:

NAME:

TEL:

CONVERSIONS

1 IN = 2.54 CM	1 IN^2 = 6.4516 CM^2
1 CM = 0.3937 IN	1 CM^2 = 0.155 IN^2
1 FT = 0.3048 M	1 FT^2 = 0.0929 M^2
1 M = 3.2808 FT	1 M^2 = 10.7639 FT^2
1 YD = 0.9144 M	1 MILE^2 = 2.59 KM^2
1 M = 1.0936 YD	1 KM^2 = 0.3861 MILES^2
1 MILE = 1.6093 KM	1 ACRE = 0.4047 HA
1 KM = 0.6214 MILES	1 HA = 2.471 ACRES
1 IN^3 = 16.387 CM^3	1 UK GAL = 4.546 L
1 CM^3 = 0.06102 IN^3	1 L = 0.22 UK GAL
1 FT^3 = 0.02832 M^3	1 OZ = 28.3495 G
1 M^3 = 35.3147 FT^3	1 G = 0.03527 OZ
1 YD^3 = 0.76456 M^3	1 LB = 453.59 G
1 M^3 = 1.30795 YD^3	1 G = 0.002205 LB
1 US GAL = 3.7854 L	1 KG = 2.2046 LB
1 L = 0.2642 US GAL	1 T (LONG) = 1016.0469 KG
1 US GAL = 0.8327 UK GAL	1 KG = 0.00098 T (LONG)

USEFUL WEBSITES

AA	THEAA.COM
RAC	RAC.CO.UK
GREEN FLAG	GREENFLAG.COM
EUROTUNNEL	EUROTUNNEL.COM
EUROSTAR	EUROSTAR.COM
LONDON TRAVEL INFO	TFL.GOV.UK
NATIONAL RAIL	NATIONALRAIL.CO.UK
NATIONAL EXPRESS COACHES	NATIONALEXPRESS.COM
BRITISH AIRWAYS	BRITISHAIRWAYS.COM
VIRGIN	VIRGINATLANTIC.COM
EASYJET	EASYJET.COM
RYANAIR	RYANAIR.COM
AVIS	AVIS.CO.UK
EUROPCAR	EUROPCAR.CO.UK
HERTZ	HERTZ.CO.UK
UK TRAFFIC INFO	NATIONALHIGHWAYS.CO.UK/TRAVEL-UPDATES
ROAD MAPS (WORLDWIDE)	GOOGLE.CO.UK/MAPS
ROAD MAPS (UK)	STREETMAP.CO.UK
WORLD TIME ZONES	WORLDTIMEZONE.COM

USEFUL CONTACTS

TOURIST INFORMATION:
WWW.VISITBRITAIN.COM
TELEPHONE: 020 7578 1000

HEALTHCARE:
WWW.NHS.UK
TELEPHONE: 111 (NON-EMERGENCY CALLS)
TELEPHONE: 999 (EMERGENCY CALLS)

POLICE:
WWW.POLICE.UK
TELEPHONE: 101 (NON-EMERGENCY CALLS)
TELEPHONE: 999 (EMERGENCY CALLS)

GOVERNMENT SERVICES:
WWW.GOV.UK

DOCTOR:

DENTIST:

HOSPITAL:

LOCAL POLICE STATION:

LOCAL COUNCIL:

MEDICAL INFORMATION:

CAR INSURANCE:

CAR BREAKDOWN:

NOTABLE DATES 2024

JANUARY
01 NEW YEAR'S DAY
02 NEW YEAR HOLIDAY (SCOTLAND)

FEBRUARY
10 CHINESE NEW YEAR (DRAGON)
13 SHROVE TUESDAY
14 VALENTINE'S DAY

MARCH
01 ST. DAVID'S DAY
08 INTERNATIONAL WOMEN'S DAY
10 MOTHER'S DAY (UK) &
    RAMADAN BEGINS
17 ST. PATRICK'S DAY
29 GOOD FRIDAY
31 EASTER SUNDAY &
    DAYLIGHT SAVING TIME STARTS

APRIL
01 EASTER MONDAY
22 PASSOVER BEGINS
23 ST. GEORGE'S DAY

MAY
06 EARLY MAY BANK HOLIDAY
27 SPRING BANK HOLIDAY

JUNE
16 FATHER'S DAY (UK)

NOTABLE DATES 202...

JULY
- 06 ISLAMIC NEW YEAR BEGINS
- 12 PUBLIC HOLIDAY (NORTHERN IRELAND)

AUGUST
- 05 SUMMER BANK HOLIDAY (SCOTLAND)
- 26 SUMMER BANK HOLIDAY (ENG, NIR, WAL)

SEPTEMBER
- 21 INTERNATIONAL DAY OF PEACE (UNITED NATIONS)

OCTOBER
- 02 ROSH HASHANAH (JEWISH NEW YEAR) BEGINS
- 10 WORLD MENTAL HEALTH DAY
- 11 YOM KIPPUR BEGINS
- 27 DAYLIGHT SAVING TIME ENDS
- 31 HALLOWEEN

NOVEMBER
- 01 DIWALI
- 05 GUY FAWKES NIGHT
- 10 REMEMBRANCE SUNDAY
- 30 ST. ANDREW'S DAY

DECEMBER
- 25 CHRISTMAS DAY
- 26 BOXING DAY
- 31 NEW YEAR'S EVE

NOTES

The Cool Garden, RHS Garden Rosemoor. © RHS Credit: RHS / Jason Ingram

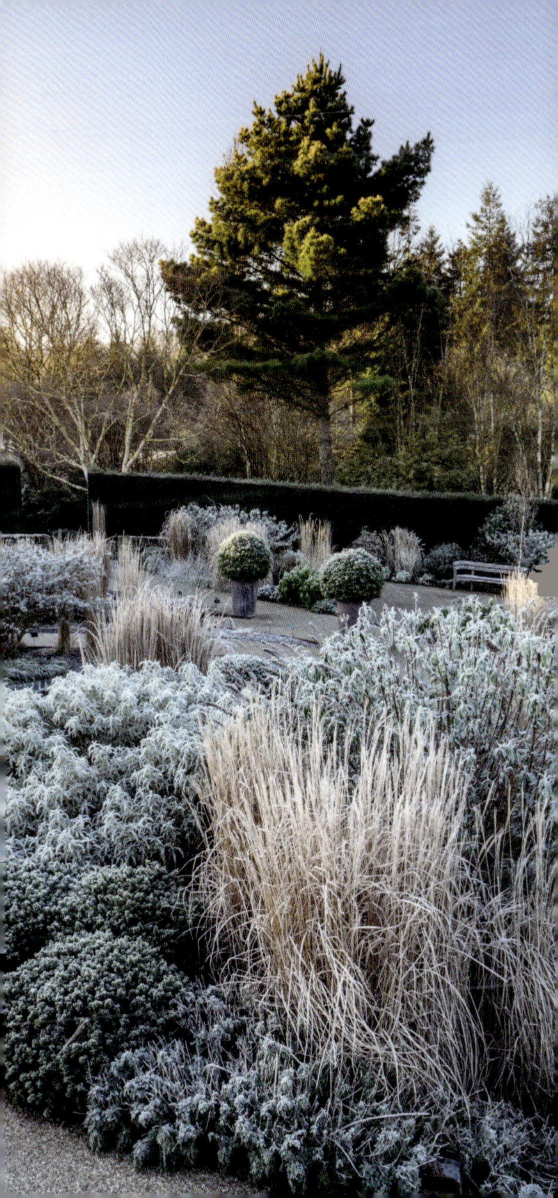

JANUARY

MONDAY
1

NEW YEAR'S DAY

TUESDAY
2

NEW YEAR HOLIDAY (SCOTLAND)

WEDNESDAY
3

THURSDAY
4

JANUARY

FRIDAY
5

SATURDAY
6

SUNDAY
7

NOTES

JANUARY

MONDAY
8

TUESDAY
9

WEDNESDAY
10

THURSDAY
11

JANUARY

FRIDAY
12

SATURDAY
13

SUNDAY
14

NOTES

JANUARY

MONDAY
15

TUESDAY
16

WEDNESDAY
17

THURSDAY
18

JANUARY

FRIDAY
19

SATURDAY
20

SUNDAY
21

NOTES

JANUARY

MONDAY
22

TUESDAY
23

WEDNESDAY
24

THURSDAY
25

JANUARY

FRIDAY
26

SATURDAY
27

SUNDAY
28

NOTES

NOTES

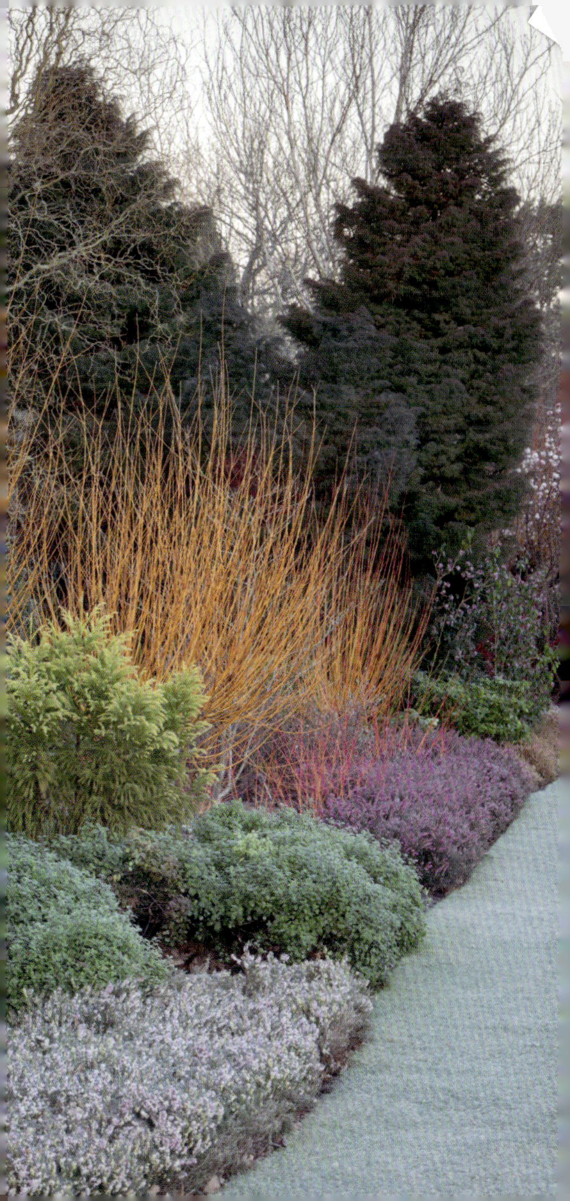

JAN/FEB

MONDAY
29

TUESDAY
30

WEDNESDAY
31

THURSDAY
1

FEBRUARY

FRIDAY
2

SATURDAY
3

SUNDAY
4

NOTES

FEBRUARY

MONDAY
5

TUESDAY
6

WEDNESDAY
7

THURSDAY
8

FEBRUARY

FRIDAY
9

SATURDAY
10

CHINESE NEW YEAR (DRAGON)

SUNDAY
11

NOTES

FEBRUARY

MONDAY
12

TUESDAY
13

SHROVE TUESDAY

WEDNESDAY
14

VALENTINE'S DAY

THURSDAY
15

FEBRUARY

FRIDAY
16

SATURDAY
17

SUNDAY
18

NOTES

FEBRUARY

MONDAY
19

TUESDAY
20

WEDNESDAY
21

THURSDAY
22

FEBRUARY

FRIDAY
23

SATURDAY
24

SUNDAY
25

NOTES

FEBRUARY

MONDAY
26

TUESDAY
27

WEDNESDAY
28

THURSDAY
29

MARCH

FRIDAY
1

ST. DAVID'S DAY

SATURDAY
2

SUNDAY
3

NOTES

NOTES

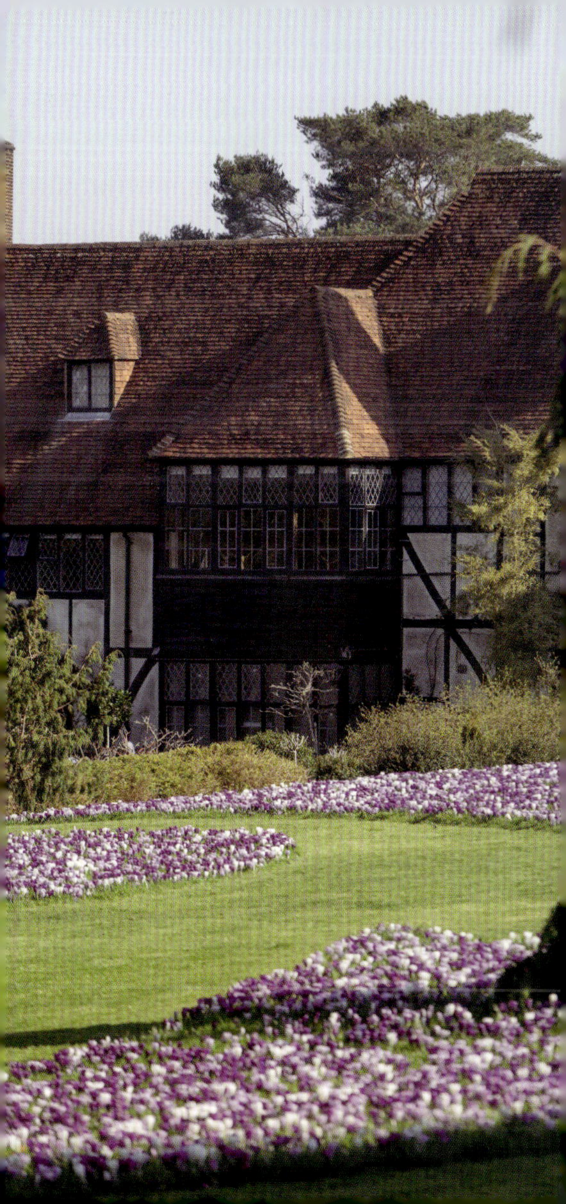

MARCH

MONDAY
4

TUESDAY
5

WEDNESDAY
6

THURSDAY
7

MARCH

FRIDAY
8

INTERNATIONAL WOMEN'S DAY

SATURDAY
9

SUNDAY
10

MOTHER'S DAY (UK) & RAMADAN BEGINS

NOTES

MARCH

MONDAY
11

TUESDAY
12

WEDNESDAY
13

THURSDAY
14

MARCH

FRIDAY
15

SATURDAY
16

SUNDAY
17

ST. PATRICK'S DAY

NOTES

MARCH

MONDAY
18

TUESDAY
19

WEDNESDAY
20

THURSDAY
21

MARCH

FRIDAY
22

SATURDAY
23

SUNDAY
24

NOTES

MARCH

MONDAY
25

TUESDAY
26

WEDNESDAY
27

THURSDAY
28

MARCH

FRIDAY
29

GOOD FRIDAY

SATURDAY
30

SUNDAY
31

EASTER SUNDAY & DAYLIGHT SAVING TIME STARTS

NOTES

NOTES

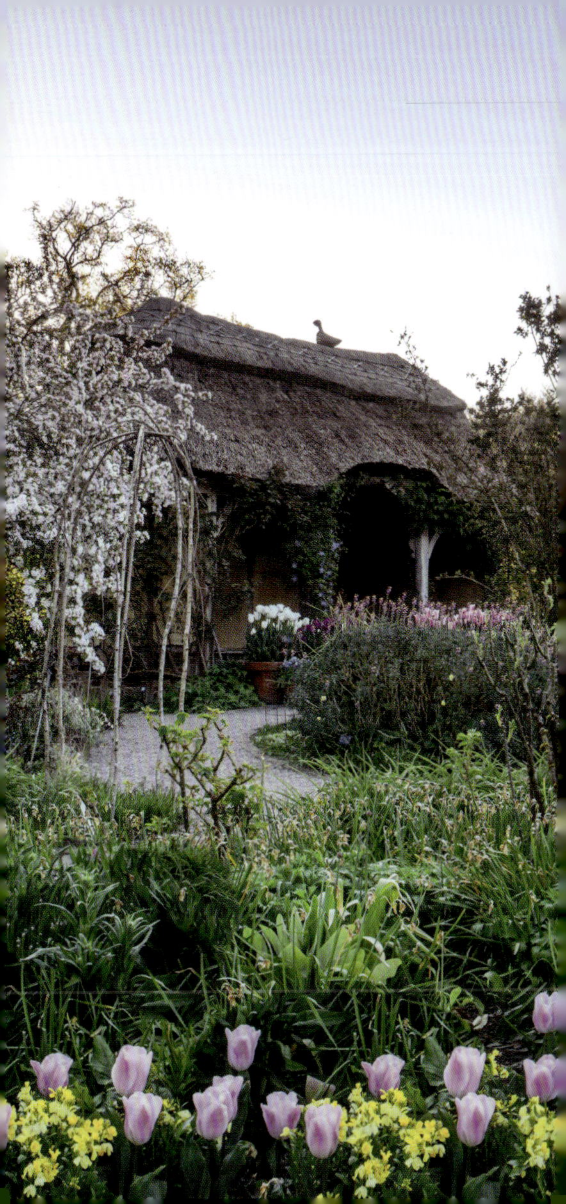

APRIL

MONDAY
1

EASTER MONDAY

TUESDAY
2

WEDNESDAY
3

THURSDAY
4

APRIL

FRIDAY
5

SATURDAY
6

SUNDAY
7

NOTES

APRIL

MONDAY
8

TUESDAY
9

WEDNESDAY
10

THURSDAY
11

APRIL

FRIDAY
12

SATURDAY
13

SUNDAY
14

NOTES

APRIL

MONDAY
15

TUESDAY
16

WEDNESDAY
17

THURSDAY
18

APRIL

FRIDAY
19

SATURDAY
20

SUNDAY
21

NOTES

APRIL

MONDAY
22

PASSOVER BEGINS
___

TUESDAY
23

ST. GEORGE'S DAY
___

WEDNESDAY
24

___

THURSDAY
25

APRIL

FRIDAY
26

SATURDAY
27

SUNDAY
28

NOTES

NOTES

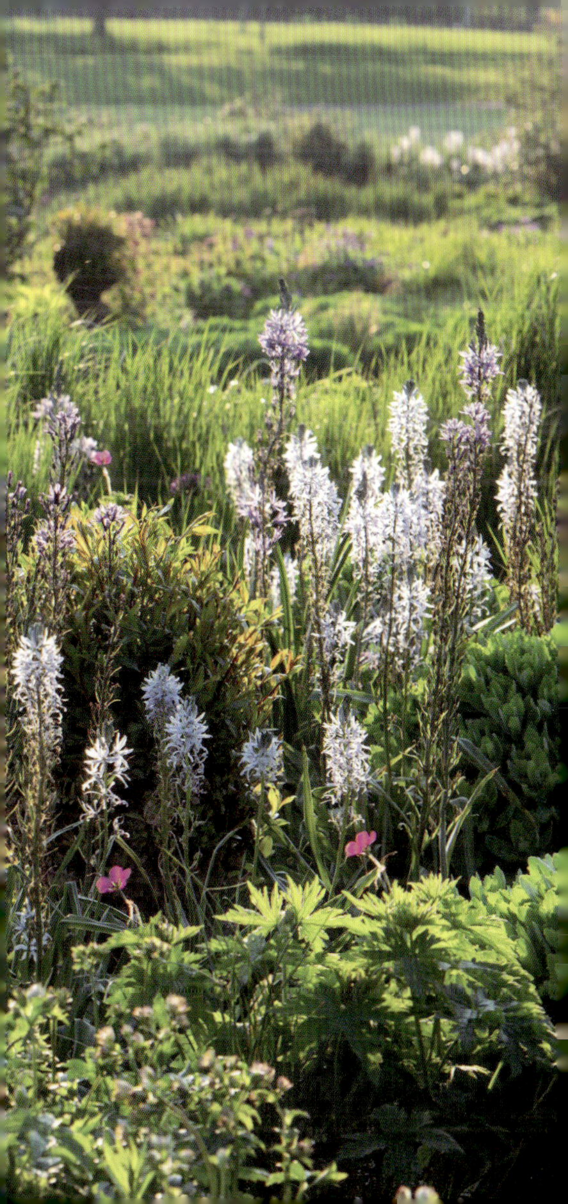

APR/MAY

MONDAY
29

TUESDAY
30

WEDNESDAY
1

THURSDAY
2

MAY

FRIDAY
3

SATURDAY
4

SUNDAY
5

NOTES

MAY

MONDAY
6

EARLY MAY BANK HOLIDAY

TUESDAY
7

WEDNESDAY
8

THURSDAY
9

MAY

FRIDAY
10

SATURDAY
11

SUNDAY
12

NOTES

MAY

MONDAY
13

TUESDAY
14

WEDNESDAY
15

THURSDAY
16

MAY

FRIDAY
17

SATURDAY
18

SUNDAY
19

NOTES

MAY

MONDAY
20

TUESDAY
21

WEDNESDAY
22

THURSDAY
23

MAY

FRIDAY
24

SATURDAY
25

SUNDAY
26

NOTES

MAY

MONDAY
27

SPRING BANK HOLIDAY

TUESDAY
28

WEDNESDAY
29

THURSDAY
30

MAY/JUN

FRIDAY
31

SATURDAY
1

SUNDAY
2

NOTES

NOTES

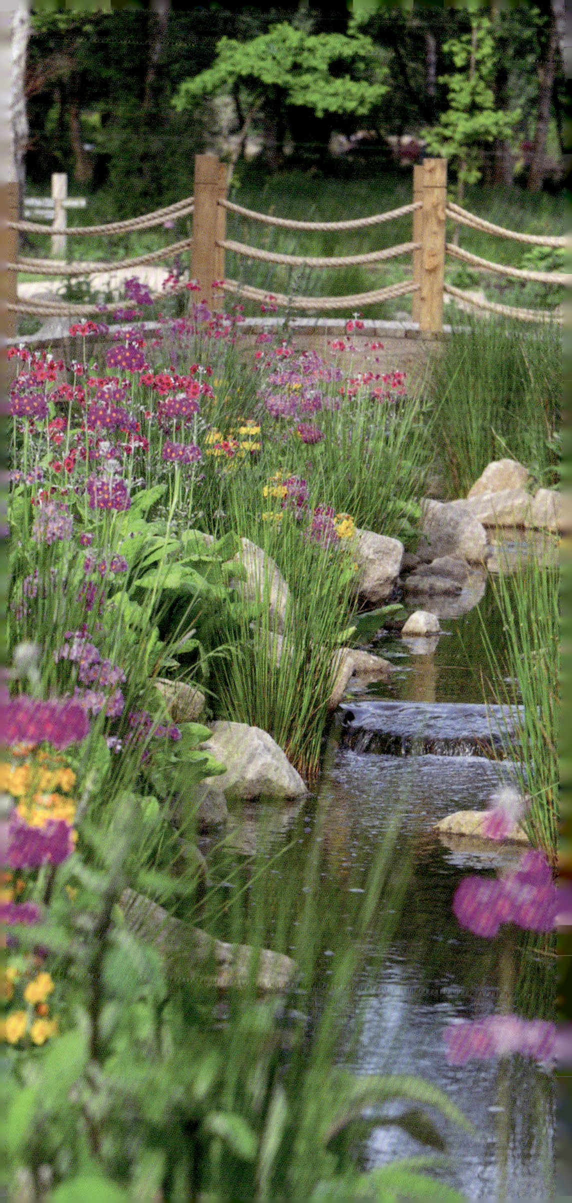

JUNE

MONDAY
3

TUESDAY
4

WEDNESDAY
5

THURSDAY
6

JUNE

FRIDAY
7

SATURDAY
8

SUNDAY
9

NOTES

JUNE

MONDAY
10

TUESDAY
11

WEDNESDAY
12

THURSDAY
13

JUNE

FRIDAY
14

SATURDAY
15

SUNDAY
16

FATHER'S DAY (UK)

NOTES

JUNE

MONDAY
17

TUESDAY
18

WEDNESDAY
19

THURSDAY
20

JUNE

FRIDAY
21

SATURDAY
22

SUNDAY
23

NOTES

JUNE

MONDAY
24

TUESDAY
25

WEDNESDAY
26

THURSDAY
27

JUNE

FRIDAY
28

SATURDAY
29

SUNDAY
30

NOTES

NOTES

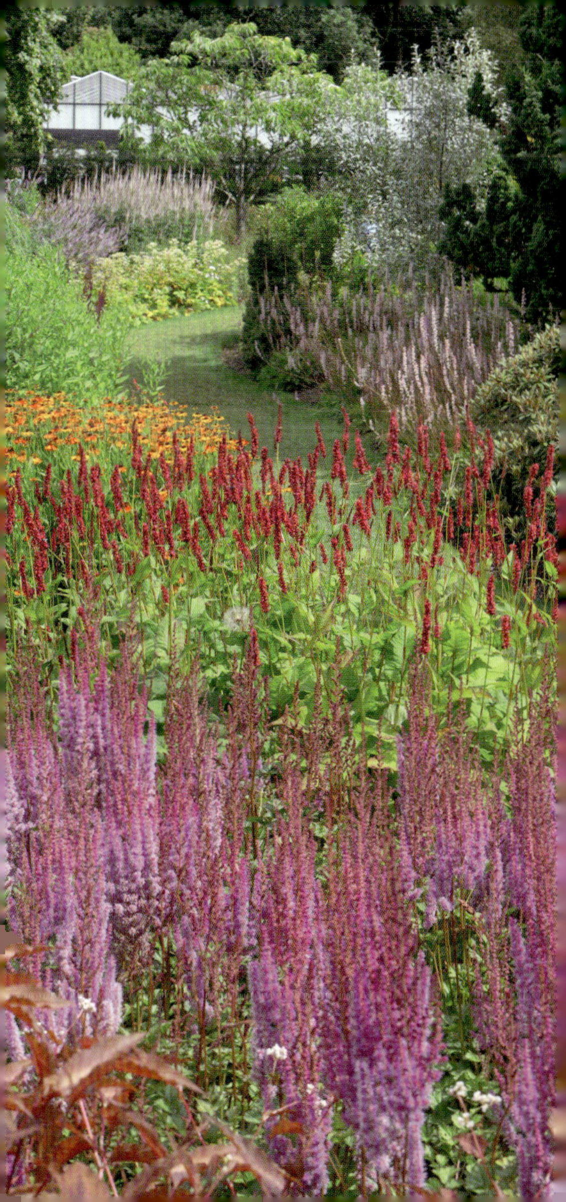

JULY

MONDAY
1

TUESDAY
2

WEDNESDAY
3

THURSDAY
4

JULY

FRIDAY
5

SATURDAY
6

ISLAMIC NEW YEAR BEGINS

SUNDAY
7

NOTES

JULY

MONDAY
8

TUESDAY
9

WEDNESDAY
10

THURSDAY
11

JULY

FRIDAY
12

PUBLIC HOLIDAY (NORTHERN IRELAND)

SATURDAY
13

SUNDAY
14

NOTES

JULY

MONDAY
15

TUESDAY
16

WEDNESDAY
17

THURSDAY
18

JULY

FRIDAY
19

SATURDAY
20

SUNDAY
21

NOTES

JULY

MONDAY
22

TUESDAY
23

WEDNESDAY
24

THURSDAY
25

JULY

FRIDAY
26

SATURDAY
27

SUNDAY
28

NOTES

NOTES

The Rose Garden, RHS Garden Hyde Hall. © RHS Credit: RHS / Richard Bloom

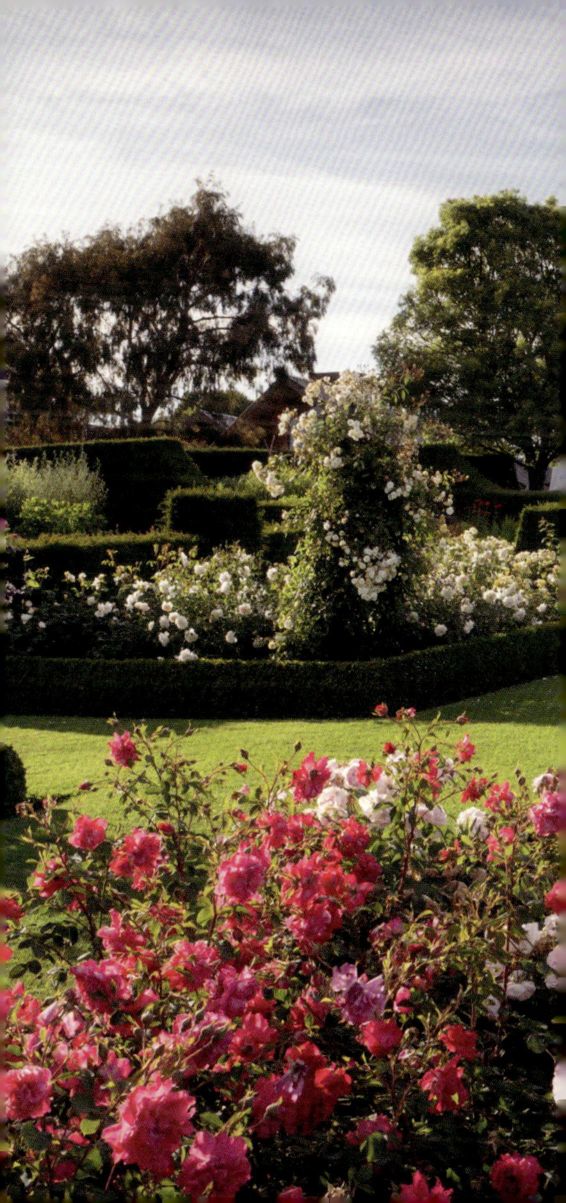

JUL/AUG

MONDAY
29

TUESDAY
30

WEDNESDAY
31

THURSDAY
1

AUGUST

FRIDAY
2

SATURDAY
3

SUNDAY
4

NOTES

AUGUST

MONDAY
5

SUMMER BANK HOLIDAY (SCOTLAND)

TUESDAY
6

WEDNESDAY
7

THURSDAY
8

AUGUST

FRIDAY
9

SATURDAY
10

SUNDAY
11

NOTES

AUGUST

MONDAY
12

TUESDAY
13

WEDNESDAY
14

THURSDAY
15

AUGUST

FRIDAY
16

SATURDAY
17

SUNDAY
18

NOTES

AUGUST

MONDAY
19

TUESDAY
20

WEDNESDAY
21

THURSDAY
22

AUGUST

FRIDAY
23

SATURDAY
24

SUNDAY
25

NOTES

AUGUST

MONDAY
26

SUMMER BANK HOLIDAY (ENG, NIR, WAL)

TUESDAY
27

WEDNESDAY
28

THURSDAY
29

AUG/SEP

FRIDAY
30

SATURDAY
31

SUNDAY
1

NOTES

NOTES

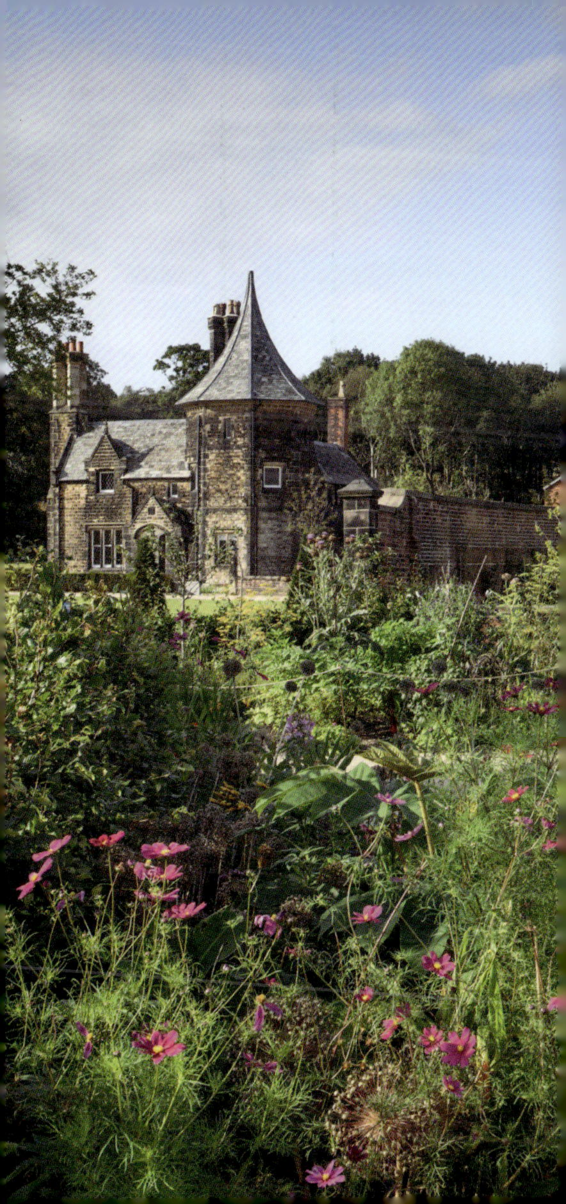

SEPTEMBER

MONDAY
2

TUESDAY
3

WEDNESDAY
4

THURSDAY
5

SEPTEMBER

FRIDAY
6

SATURDAY
7

SUNDAY
8

NOTES

SEPTEMBER

MONDAY
9

TUESDAY
10

WEDNESDAY
11

THURSDAY
12

SEPTEMBER

FRIDAY
13

SATURDAY
14

SUNDAY
15

NOTES

SEPTEMBER

MONDAY
16

TUESDAY
17

WEDNESDAY
18

THURSDAY
19

SEPTEMBER

FRIDAY
20

SATURDAY
21

INTERNATIONAL DAY OF PEACE (UNITED NATIONS)

SUNDAY
22

NOTES

SEPTEMBER

MONDAY
23

TUESDAY
24

WEDNESDAY
25

THURSDAY
26

SEPTEMBER

FRIDAY
27

SATURDAY
28

SUNDAY
29

NOTES

NOTES

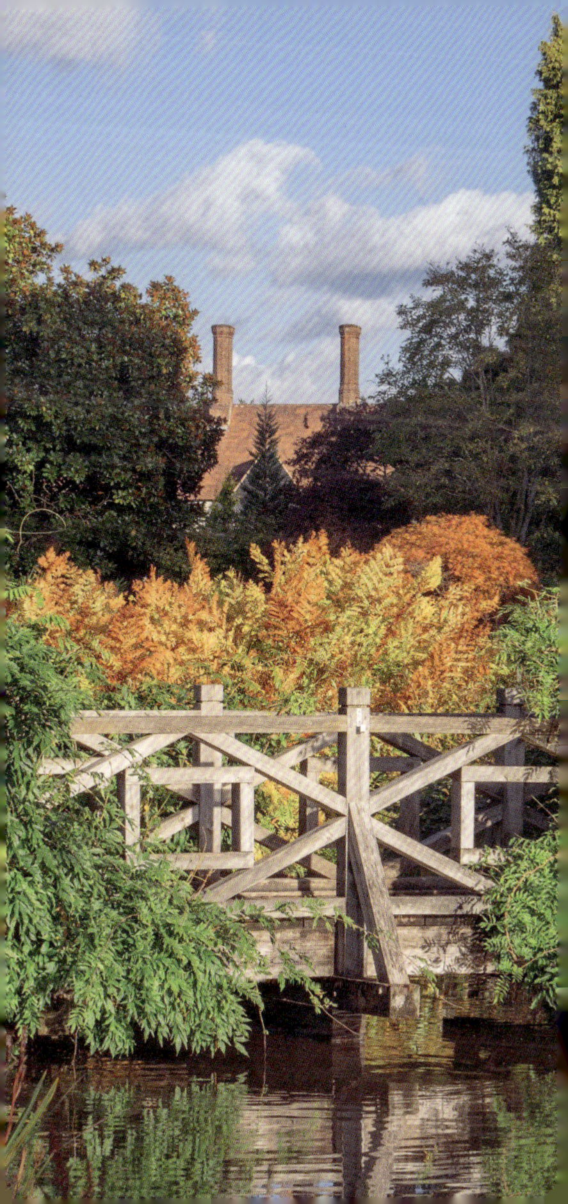

SEP/OCT

MONDAY
30

TUESDAY
1

WEDNESDAY
2

ROSH HASHANAH (JEWISH NEW YEAR) BEGINS

THURSDAY
3

OCTOBER

FRIDAY
4

SATURDAY
5

SUNDAY
6

NOTES

OCTOBER

MONDAY
7

TUESDAY
8

WEDNESDAY
9

THURSDAY
10

WORLD MENTAL HEALTH DAY

OCTOBER

FRIDAY
11

YOM KIPPUR BEGINS

SATURDAY
12

SUNDAY
13

NOTES

OCTOBER

MONDAY
14

TUESDAY
15

WEDNESDAY
16

THURSDAY
17

OCTOBER

FRIDAY
18

SATURDAY
19

SUNDAY
20

NOTES

OCTOBER

MONDAY
21

TUESDAY
22

WEDNESDAY
23

THURSDAY
24

OCTOBER

FRIDAY
25

SATURDAY
26

SUNDAY
27

DAYLIGHT SAVING TIME ENDS

NOTES

OCTOBER

MONDAY
28

TUESDAY
29

WEDNESDAY
30

THURSDAY
31

HALLOWEEN

NOVEMBER

FRIDAY
1

DIWALI

SATURDAY
2

SUNDAY
3

NOTES

NOTES

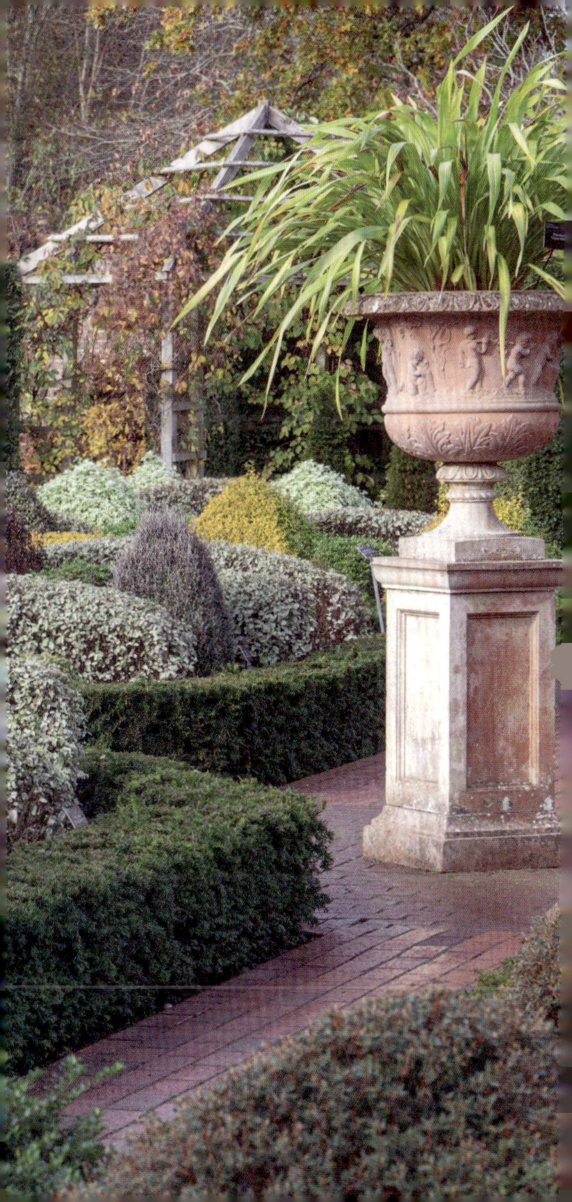

NOVEMBER

MONDAY
4

TUESDAY
5

GUY FAWKES NIGHT

WEDNESDAY
6

THURSDAY
7

NOVEMBER

FRIDAY
8

SATURDAY
9

SUNDAY
10

REMEMBRANCE SUNDAY

NOTES

NOVEMBER

MONDAY
11

TUESDAY
12

WEDNESDAY
13

THURSDAY
14

NOVEMBER

FRIDAY
15

SATURDAY
16

SUNDAY
17

NOTES

NOVEMBER

MONDAY
18

TUESDAY
19

WEDNESDAY
20

THURSDAY
21

NOVEMBER

FRIDAY
22

SATURDAY
23

SUNDAY
24

NOTES

NOVEMBER

MONDAY
25

TUESDAY
26

WEDNESDAY
27

THURSDAY
28

NOV/DEC

FRIDAY
29

SATURDAY
30

ST. ANDREW'S DAY

SUNDAY
1

NOTES

NOTES

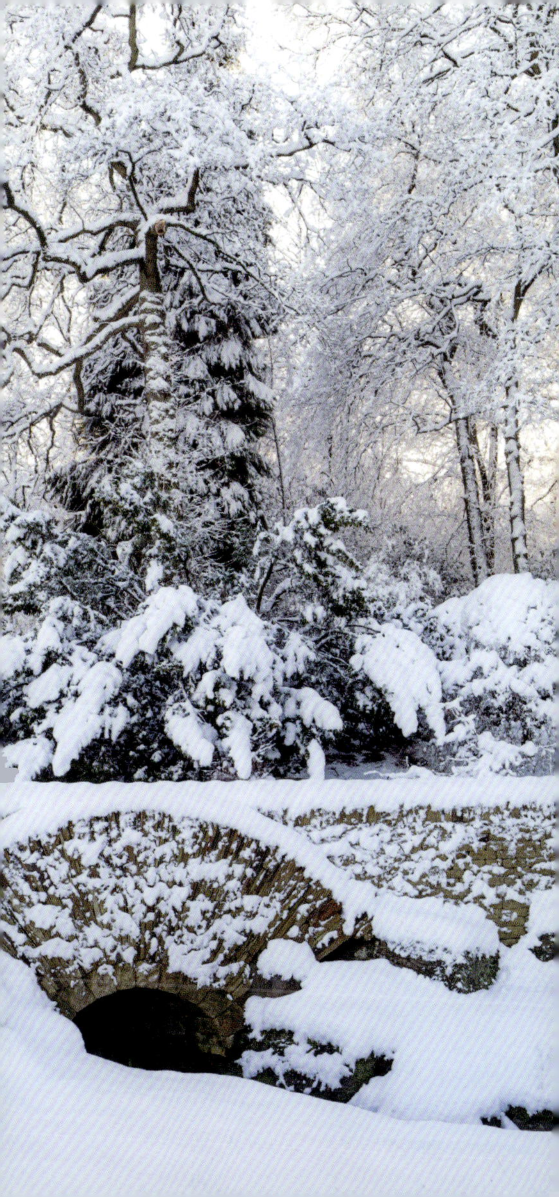

DECEMBER

MONDAY
2

TUESDAY
3

WEDNESDAY
4

THURSDAY
5

DECEMBER

FRIDAY
6

SATURDAY
7

SUNDAY
8

NOTES

DECEMBER

MONDAY
9

TUESDAY
10

WEDNESDAY
11

THURSDAY
12

DECEMBER

FRIDAY
13

SATURDAY
14

SUNDAY
15

NOTES

DECEMBER

MONDAY
16

TUESDAY
17

WEDNESDAY
18

THURSDAY
19

DECEMBER

FRIDAY
20

SATURDAY
21

SUNDAY
22

NOTES

DECEMBER

MONDAY
23

TUESDAY
24

WEDNESDAY
25

CHRISTMAS DAY

THURSDAY
26

BOXING DAY

DECEMBER

FRIDAY
27

SATURDAY
28

SUNDAY
29

NOTES

DEC '24/JAN '25

MONDAY
30

TUESDAY
31

NEW YEAR'S EVE

WEDNESDAY
1

NEW YEAR'S DAY

THURSDAY
2

NEW YEAR HOLIDAY (SCOTLAND)

JANUARY '25

FRIDAY
3

SATURDAY
4

SUNDAY
5

NOTES

IMPORTANT DATES

IMPORTANT DATES

ADDRESS & TELEPHONE

NAME:

ADDRESS:

POSTCODE:

TELEPHONE:

WORK:

MOBILE:

FAX:

E-MAIL:

NAME:

ADDRESS:

POSTCODE:

TELEPHONE:

WORK:

MOBILE:

FAX:

E-MAIL:

ADDRESS & TELEPHONE

NAME:

ADDRESS:

POSTCODE:

TELEPHONE:

WORK:

MOBILE:

FAX:

E-MAIL:

NAME:

ADDRESS:

POSTCODE:

TELEPHONE:

WORK:

MOBILE:

FAX:

E-MAIL:

NOTES

NOTES

Herbaceous Border, RHS Garden Hyde Hall. © RHS Credit: RHS / Joanna Kossak